Dream Number 4

An inspirational book to help you fulfill <u>Your</u> Dreams!

By
Brenette Wilder

Published by Purpose Publishing
1503 Main Street #168
Grandview, MO 64030
Website: www.purpose-publishing.com
Email: administrator@purpose-publishing.com

Copyright © 2009 by Brenette Wilder

Cover designed by Aaron Norris
Inside photographs by Paul Catlett
Editing by Benita Ugoline and Sheryl Fleming

Inquiries may be addressed to: www.dreamnumber4.com

All rights reserved. No portion of this book may be reproduced, stored in a retrieval system, or transmitted in any form or by any means – electronic, mechanical, photocopy, recording, or any other without the prior permission of the author.

All poems are from the author, unless otherwise noted. All scriptures are from the King James Version and New Living Translation, unless otherwise noted.

ISBN: 978-0-615-33336-6

This book is dedicated to Catera, Christina, Charleen, and Cleotis to remember that God has a plan for our life.

Thoughts from the Author

A fantastic thing about the deliberateness of God's purpose is it fulfills just what it sets out to do. Once active, purpose cannot be stopped; it cannot remain a contemplation of the past. It goes forth revealing importance to whom it is intended. And, it enlightens our understanding for permanent life changes in the areas of salvation, deliverance, forgiveness, and more.

So doesn't it make sense for us to make our dreams align with God's purpose? Take a minute to pause and reflect inward to seek counsel from God, the owner of the dream. Remember that you are born of the Spirit of God and His Spirit will guide you in your understanding. Don't reject his plan for your life…accept it! Receive God's plan and make it uniquely significant. Urge your dream into action by allowing your confidence to match the faith God made available for you. And finally, be the difference in the world with newness in how you think and live your dream.

Start now. During your prayer time, read the scriptures below that have reference to "dream" and "purpose."

- Daniel 1:17 God gave these four young men an unusual aptitude for learning the literature and science of the time. And God gave Daniel special ability in understanding the meanings of visions and <u>dreams</u>.

- Acts 26:16 Now stand up! <u>For I have appeared to you to appoint you as my servant and my witness</u>. You are to tell the world about this experience and about other times I will appear to you.

- Matthew 2:13 Now when they had gone, behold, an angel of the Lord appeared to Joseph in a <u>dream</u> and said, "Get up! Take the Child and His mother and flee to Egypt, and remain there until I tell you; for Herod is going to search for the Child to destroy Him."

- Luke 7:30 But the Pharisees and the lawyers rejected God's <u>purpose</u> for themselves, not having been baptized by John.

- Genesis 28:12 As he slept, he <u>dreamed</u> of a stairway that reached from earth to heaven. And he saw the angels of God going up and down on it.

How to Read This Book

Each chapter has a main thought that describes the author's experience in fulfilling her dream. The author leaves space at the end of each chapter for comments. Also, a personal poem written by the author (unless otherwise noted) and a scripture relevant to each chapter follow the comment section.

> Joseph's dream was added on the side margin for the reader's personal reflection and comparison to his/her own dream.

The space is left below for comments:

_____

_____

_____

_____

A poem is at the end of each chapter
Scripture: Eph 3:17
      And I pray that Christ …

✦ Table of Contents ✦

Introduction:	....	8
Chapter 1:	Resurrected Dream...............................	11
Chapter 2:	Wishing Won't Make Your Dreams Happen...	23
Chapter 3:	The Main Ingredient......................................	38
Chapter 4:	The Voice, the Hunger, the List....................	47
Chapter 5:	Dream Fear Factors.......................................	56
Chapter 6:	Don't Waste Time	62
Chapter 7:	Opportunity, Not Failure...............................	68
Chapter 8:	Teamwork...	73
Chapter 9:	Give Thanks...	79
Chapter 10:	To Share or Not to Share................................	84
Chapter 11:	Searching..	87
Chapter 12:	What's Next?...	90

✧ Introduction ✧

This book is written to fulfill Dream Number 4 on a list I created at a women's retreat. I had long forgotten about the list until I heard my daughter's discussion with her dad involving the never-ending "why" questions. Anyone with kids has heard them on numerous occasions. Dad, "How old were you when …?" "How did you and mom meet?" "How are babies made?" The questions go on and on, and just when you can't stand another question they ask the big one. They ask the one question that stops you dead in your tracks. For each person that big question may be different. It may be one question you don't have an answer to, or the one question you hoped no one would ever ask, or even the one question you never asked yourself or considered. Dad, she asked, "Why didn't you become a lawyer?" Sounds like a simple enough question. But, on the sidelines observing the whole thing, I rephrased the question in my mind this way: Why did you stop short of accomplishing the single most important thing you dreamed of becoming?

My husband's dream of becoming a lawyer started when he was a young boy, somewhere around 13 years of age. His uncle's subtle, but insightful hints that he would make a great lawyer were successful in making him dream big. His dream of becoming a lawyer continued throughout college, but when life became challenging with fatigue and personal problems he lost his focus. He lost his dream.

This question of lost dreams is hardly limited to my husband. I could have easily looked at my own life to see ideas and dreams not brought to fruition. But who is to blame? I pointed my finger at my job and my family, but mostly at my life for being too busy with "self-assigned stuff." The truth was I couldn't blame anyone but myself. And no one but me could take the first steps towards changing the situation…making my own dreams come alive.

Now I am on track with purpose and power! This time something different is motivating me to push forward: A deeper hunger and God's confirmation to proceed. It is my hope that my story will cause a dreamers' epidemic. I want everyone reading this to become motivated enough to move themselves and others past neutral into drive and get their dreams moving again.

Chapter 1
Resurrected Dream

 didn't know at the time, but several events would be used to reinforce a strong urge I felt to write my story. The first event occurred while working on a community project. I became keenly aware of people and my circumstances. All around me, one word stood out that catapulted me into action - "Dream."

I have always loved working on community projects. It's the one place where I have seen lives transformed, not on the surface or materially, but on the inside. A natural and effortless change occurs provoked by a gesture of love and the move

> *Genesis 37*
>
> [1]And Jacob dwelt in the land wherein his father was a stranger, in the land of Canaan.

Genesis 37

²These are the generations of Jacob. Joseph, being seventeen years old, was feeding the flock with his brethren; and the lad was with the sons of Bilhah, and with the sons of Zilpah, his father's wives: and Joseph brought unto his father their evil report.

of the Holy Spirit. In this moment, it doesn't really matter how eloquent your delivery is or how passionate you are about your work. Because, when someone is hurting or lost they are not turning to you for help they are turning to God. And do you know what's really amazing? God is keenly aware of human behavior and is sovereign; as He is pulling that hurting person out of the trenches his overflowing love can transform your life and your outlook on service.

The turning point in this day began as I was multitasking. I made a trip to the library with two purposes: to look for personal reading material and to see if the library had juvenile books for sale that could be used in my project. With my books in hand and a brief feeling of satisfaction with my selections, I approached the check out counter and overheard a girl standing next to me searching for information related to "erratic dreams." I was startled to hear her request after recently praying to God about my dream list. In hindsight, her quest to find some type of conscious insight into her dreams to make sense of them was similar to my own thoughts of how to make sense of my dreams for life.

> **Genesis 37**
>
> [3] Now Israel loved Joseph more than all his children, because he was the son of his old age: and he made him a coat of many colours.

Reflecting back, it's amazing how my own dreams even survived my childhood. Hard work and poverty hung around like an overambitious friend. Poverty alone can consume and smother out all hope. Each day took sheer willpower by my mother to continually press onward. The gateway to her success of overcoming poverty was

> **Genesis 37**
>
> ⁴And when his brethren saw that their father loved him more than all his brethren, they hated him, and could not speak peaceably unto him.

fueled as she demolished each road block — upgrading from a wood burning cooking stove to a gas stove; washing clothes with running water instead of rainwater collected in barrels; warming the home with central heating instead of a wood heater; and the pure enjoyment of indoor plumbing instead of an outhouse. Thanks to God, our experiences are not wasted. Every experience is used to make a stronger you and a stronger faith that adds value to the family of believers. Hold tight to your dreams. Don't give up on yourself. I believe a dream given to you by God will have longevity through your struggles. How God does this is beyond me, but Isaiah 55:11 (NLT) says: "It is the same with my word. I send it out, and it always produces fruit. It will accomplish all I want it to, and it will prosper everywhere I send it". And I am thankful His word does.

The second event that catapulted me into action happened after I left the library and went to the grocery store. Standing in the checkout line, I picked-up a magazine that featured a story on the front cover entitled, "Dream Big—How to Let Yourself Get What You Want." Within minutes of reading the title, I dismissed any doubts that this was merely a coincidence. And just as quickly as I accepted the idea, I started to reject it. I thought, "Is God revealing an assignment to me? Is this real?" I began to smile as though I had heard a joke.

Many times I have asked God to show me just one sign. So why is it when he does

Genesis 37

[5]And Joseph dreamed a dream, and he told it his brethren: and they hated him yet the more.

> **Genesis 37**
>
> ⁶And he said unto them, Hear, I pray you, this dream which I have dreamed:

just that, I laugh? What will it take for us to see the bread crumbs God leaves for us to follow? Mankind has been searching for centuries to find evidence of God's existence and when He seeks us out we run scared; dodging Him with our intellect and knowledge. Each day He works out our failures and successes' giving us the opportunity to do what pleases Him. When you really think about it, God has been working on us our whole life; preparing us to fulfill the dream He gave and to live out our purpose.

The final event involving a sign from God occurred after returning home. Before going to bed I went to the basement to rummage through boxes containing my children's juvenile Christian books. I wanted to donate them to the community project. I noticed a book with Martin Luther King's picture on it and decided to keep the book for future reading. Heading upstairs after organizing the books for the project, it dawned on me that I should go back and read the book's title. Going down the steps with great excitement, I knew God was giving me another chance. Reading the book's title, "I have a Dream," confirmed without a doubt within my spirit that this was not a mere coincidence. Everything became clear. God wanted my voice, my story, and He wanted me to fulfill my dreams; beginning with Dream Number 4 to write this book. Wow! How awesome God is!!! This was my assignment. And my greatest reward would be for you to fulfill your dreams and "write"

> *Genesis 37*
>
> [7]For, behold, we were binding sheaves in the field, and, lo, my sheaf arose, and also stood upright; and, behold, your sheaves stood round about, and made obeisance to my sheaf.

Genesis 37

[8]And his brethren said to him, Shalt thou indeed reign over us? Or shalt thou indeed have dominion over us? And they hated him yet the more for his dreams, and for his words.

your own success story.

Inexperienced and insecure about my ability to write, I plunged into a new world. I had no business plan, no experience, and no initial support from family, just the unrevealed plan of God. This feeling reminded me of when I went off to college my freshmen year, the first day starting a new job, the first time giving birth to a baby, and even the first day I went to see my brother during the time he was dying of cancer. The feeling was fear and it did not discriminate. It manifested itself in every part of my body. In each "first time" situation, I didn't know how things would shape up. I had butterflies that lasted a few days, and no matter how hard I tried the fear just didn't go away until I was fully submerged in the experience and had one option: God.

As God resurrected my dream of publishing a book, I looked forward to learning more about myself. Learning what I am really made of, and if I had what my mom, mother-in-law, grandmothers, older sisters, and aunts had – strength, courage, and tenacity. I wanted to have courage to press into God and continue forward in my trials and responsibilities regardless how difficult they became. I wanted to glean from my female relatives how to stay focused and on track. I wanted to remember how they took nothing and made something from it. I wanted to be able to look a challenge straight on and say: With God I can do everything.

I hope this book inspires you to

> **Genesis 37**
>
> [9]And he dreamed yet another dream, and told it his brethren, and said, Behold, I have dreamed a dream more; and, behold, the sun and the moon and the eleven stars made obeisance to me.

Genesis 37

[10] And he told it to his father, and to his brethren: and his father rebuked him, and said unto him, what is this dream that thou hast dreamed? Shall I and thy mother and thy brethren indeed come to bow down ourselves to thee to the earth?

remember the dreams you tucked away, thinking that they would never happen. Now is the time for your confidence to fully match the faith God has available for you. Now is the time to re-evaluate your future and ask yourself: How can I dream again? How can I resurrect the dreams that I gave up on long ago? Who can I partner with or who can mentor me in this journey?

If you are willing, get ready for working in the realm of the unknown. Join me and let's go!

Make a dream list by answering the three questions on the previous page.

Genesis 37

[11]And his brethren envied him; but his father observed the saying.

Seen With the Eyes of My Heart
Brenette Wilder

Genesis 37

¹²And his brethren went to feed their father's flock in Shechem.

Scripture: Eph 3:17
And I pray that Christ will be more and more at home in your hearts as you trust in him. May your roots go down deep into the soil of God's marvelous love.

It's a dream from long ago
A dream of promise
Selective with words binding
Seen with the eyes of my heart

It was a dream of things to come
A promise of love
A promise of purpose
A promise of completion
Seen with the eyes of my heart

It is no longer I who live it
But my Savior through me
Manifested for you and me
Seen with the eyes of my heart

It's a dream from long ago
And the fulfillment for today
Seen with the eyes of my heart
The eyes of my heart

Chapter 2
Wishing Won't Make Your Dreams Happen

Genesis 37

[13] And Israel said unto Joseph, Do not thy brethren feed the flock in Shechem? come, and I will send thee unto them. And he said to him, here am I.

This day began like any other day. The struggle to get out of bed was difficult. I attempted to open my eyes followed by a second attempt to get up. I forced myself to my feet. Hypnotically, I walk to the adjourning room, a place that I have come to make my own quiet space. This is a place where the deepest desires of my heart are made known to God, who is all too familiar with them. He listens and I am free and open with Him. Sometimes I don't know what to pray for. I feel empty as I struggle through my prayers, but this time I am focused and I asked God the same

> **Genesis 37**
>
> [14]And he said to him, Go, I pray thee, see whether it be well with thy brethren, and well with the flocks; and bring me word again. So he sent him out of the vale of Hebron, and he came to Shechem.

question I have asked on previous occasions: "Will I ever fulfill the dreams of my heart?" Several questions came to mind: "Am I too old? Do I lack motivation? Am I committed enough?" The tiny voice in my head said, "You've tried once, even twice, and you couldn't make it work then. So what makes this day any different? God, what makes this day any different, I thought again? How can I ever move from thinking and wishing about my elusive dreams to acting and planning enduring dreams?" This time I directed my frustration towards the Holy Spirit. "If it is your job to guide and lead me, then why can't I hear you?" I thought with megaphone intensity. Totally frustrated, I needed to hear from God. I knew that the voice of self doubt in my head was not from God. Satan was using my weakness to plant snares and stumbling blocks strategically in the right places to trip me up. But it was through prayer that the Holy Spirit reminded me that I must stay close to hear his voice over the voice of Satan. Not only did the Holy Spirit answer me, but he put the blame where it should have been - on me. Maybe you haven't been frustrated in your situation before, but I have. There is nothing you can't ask God. He can handle honesty and tough questions. At the heart of tough questions is an individual seeking to know a situation, a person, or God better.

   To be victorious in finding an answer to your questions, God has given his Word and the Holy Spirit to lead, guide, teach, help, and

> **Genesis 37**
>
> [15] And a certain man found him, and, beholds, he was wandering in the field: and the man asked him, saying, what seekest thou?

> **Genesis 37**
>
> ¹⁶And he said, I seek my brethren: tell me, I pray thee, where they feed their flocks.

convict. In this moment of clarity, I asked the Holy Spirit to be my team leader in this quest. The ground rules were set in the Bible and I needed to follow them. I reminded myself that as my leader, the Holy Spirit didn't just show up to be my best friend when I wanted to hang out. He wanted to fellowship and exercise my spiritual muscles daily. He was not to be treated as some entity connected by strings that I could force, guide, or move into a position I wanted Him to be. The Bible says the Spirit of God was present at the beginning of creation, hovering over the waters (Gen 1:2). He operates in the life of the believer to make sure that the thoughts of God are revealed and taught: "Men spoke from God as they were carried along by the Holy Spirit" (II Peter 1:21). He is omnipresent: "Where can I go from your Spirit? Where can I flee from your presence" (Psalms 139:7-10)? He is omnipotent: "The Holy Spirit will come upon you and the power of the Most High will over shadow you" (Luke 1:35).

The Holy Spirit being equal to God required a higher standard of relationship than being an invisible friend. So, when I approached the Holy Spirit, I needed to maintain a posture of submission before Him. His presence is not designed to make me feel or look good, but rather to reveal God's thoughts to me; convict me to change a negative behavior or action in a manner that will attract others to God; please God, and show the truth in all situations. My maturity to hear and to be submissive and my willingness to go would be essential for my success.

Genesis 37

[17]And the man said, they are departed hence; for I heard them say, Let us go to Dothan. And Joseph went after his brethren, and found them in Dothan.

Genesis 37

¹⁸And when they saw him afar off, even before he came near unto them, they conspired against him to slay him.

Hebrews 5:14 says, "But solid food is for the mature, for those whose faculties have been trained by practice to distinguish good from evil."

When I was young it was hard to understand the language of mature Christian women. Submerged in the middle of grown-up talk, I overheard some personal insights like — the Holy Spirit lead me around unseen danger, the Spirit placed you on my mind, or even the Holy Spirit directed me to do this or that. From a child's point of view, understanding the Holy Spirit seemed impossible. This was mainly because I couldn't hear the audible instructions that the Holy Spirit was giving. I thought his voice was limited to a certain group.

As an adult, I know that the Holy Spirit

does speak to you. He speaks through your circumstances, the Bible, individuals, and He uses many other methods and tools available to Him to communicate the thoughts of God. By spending time with the Holy Spirit, I am learning to recognize His voice. Now instead of rushing in to control every situation, I want to be controlled and under the control of the Holy Spirit. I need my tongue, my actions, my temper, my heart, and my life controlled by something greater than myself, because deep within me is an old nature that is self-centered, prideful, and has a poor sense of judgment. I needed to know God's truth about my life. How I should worship and serve Him, and how I should go about fulfilling my dreams.

> **Genesis 37**
>
> [19]And they said one to another, Behold, this dreamer cometh.

It was an old custom during church

Genesis 37

²⁰Come now therefore, and let us slay him, and cast him into some pit, and we will say, some evil beast hath devoured him: and we shall see what will become of his dreams.

revival for the Pastor to invite unbelievers to the front pew called the mourner's bench. The mourner's bench was set aside for candidates to receive confirmation and salvation. During this period you prayed, fasted, and read the Bible expecting to receive understanding of the Bible and confirmation that God heard your prayer of salvation or deliverance. I believe this custom was designed to be a sacred moment as well as a supernatural experience. The awareness of God's presence, his reaffirming love, the joy of forgiveness, the cleansing of sin – it's all experienced during this custom. It's not just a moment for the candidate, but the whole family rallies around the individual in prayer. No coaxing or interaction with friends or family is allowed.

You isolate yourself submerging yourself into full-time prayer and meditation. Even though today we know that this custom is not required for the purpose of salvation, we still look to our Father to confirm what we do.

> **Genesis 37**
>
> [21]And Reuben heard it, and he delivered him out of their hands; and said, Let us not kill him.

This time His confirmation is the one thing that would move me into action. Throughout the week I pondered my dreams. I wanted to wait on God to salvage them and transform them into something great. As I waited, and read Proverbs, I realized God wanted me to be successful in everything I do. He wants my life to be a reflection of Him and His ways. (Commit your works to the Lord and your thoughts will be established Proverb 16:3.)

    How was I going to express God and bring Him glory in what I did? If the truth

Genesis 37

²²And Reuben said unto them, Shed no blood, but cast him into this pit that is in the wilderness, and lay no hand upon him; that he might rid him out of their hands, to deliver him to his father again.

was told, until now my dreams only shone a light on myself. That type of self-gratification kept God out of the picture.

How often I have pushed – no, bulldozed my way through life, leaving the Holy Spirit on the roadside only to be reported as a spiritual hit and run. This time I would stick around for the report to be written up and submitted to the proper authority for mercy. I wanted the report to say that I was granted a full grace approval to proceed.

This approval was reinforced while listening to a television program featuring the life of Jackie Joyner Kersee. The reporter stated that she was one of the greatest heptathlon competitors of all time. In the program, one of her friends revealed that after losing an Olympic gold medal, she vowed, "I will never again let me defeat myself."

That clinched it for me. All that time, I had been my own worst enemy. My mind and my body were fighting against my deepest desires. Tension in my life and voices from other people constantly reminded me of the challenges ahead paralyzed me from moving forward. Before I could retaliate I was captured and imprisoned in fear. I stopped moving forward and I became comfortable with self-inflicted lost.

This is my advice to you. Keep your focus on God. Learn from your setbacks. One knockdown doesn't mean you can't get up and hit the reset button for a fresh start. Continue to keep active and pray to God for

Genesis 37

[23] And it came to pass, when Joseph was come unto his brethren, that they strip Joseph out of his coat, his coat of many colours that was on him;

Genesis 37

²⁴And they took him, and cast him into a pit: and the pit was empty, there was no water in it.

guidance and let Him be in control of fulfilling your dream(s).

Things to consider:

Answer the questions in the space below. Why is being in control so important? Who is really in control?

_____

_____

_____

_____

What dreams would you like to accomplish within the next five years? What's stopping you?

_____

_____

_____

_____

Identify roadblocks that are preventing you from achieving your dream(s).

What must you eliminate in order to satisfy your dream(s)?

_____
_____
_____
_____
_____
_____
_____
_____
_____
_____
_____
_____

Genesis 37

²⁵ And they sat down to eat bread: and they lifted up their eyes and looked, and, behold, a company of Ishmaelite came from Gilead with their camels bearing spicery and balm and myrrh, going to carry it down to Egypt.

Listening for your voice
Brenette Wilder

Genesis 37

²⁶And Judah said unto his brethren, what profit is it if we slay our brother, and conceal his blood?

Scripture: Philippians 4:13
I can do everything through Him who gives me strength.

It has to be your words Lord
It has to come from you
I'm listening for your voice
But I hear only mine

In the silence, You say ...

Lift up your soul
You can trust me
You can hope in me all day long
You will not cause me to be ashamed

I say...

Show me how
Teach me your ways
Help me to believe and not to sway

You say...

Repent and forgive
Clean your ugly stain
Restore yourself again
And let me be the watchmen over you again

Side Bar Conversation

One day while my daughter was looking at television (the background music was romantic and the scene touching), she said with great sincerity: "I wish I could hear music in my life". I agreed with her. How great it would be to have your life enhanced by strings, wind, and percussion instruments that translated the exact emotion you were feeling. But, the Holy Spirit is the background music in our lives; setting the tempo and pace, guiding us through life with warnings, cautions, and love. An arrangement composed with our personal DNA stamped all over it.

Genesis 37

[27] Come, and let us sell him to the Ishmaelite, and let not our hand be upon him; for he is our brother and our flesh. And his brethren were content.

Chapter 3
The Main Ingredient

Genesis 37

²⁸Then there passed by Midianites merchantmen; and they drew and lifted up Joseph out of the pit, and sold Joseph to the Ishmaelite for twenty pieces of silver: and they brought Joseph into Egypt.

s a youngster, I didn't think about writing a book. At least it wasn't anywhere close to being my favorite top five things to do. You see, I thought like most youngsters I was automatically destined to accomplish my dreams, and foolishly I thought it wouldn't take much effort to achieve them.

While growing up in the 60's, it didn't matter that I lived in a four room home. It didn't matter that the bathroom was really an outhouse or that the water for washing clothes was really rainwater. Somehow God didn't fully reveal to me my poverty stricken environment. I imagined that I could do anything. Singing for Motown, being a ballerina, and working in corporate America were the visions that danced around in my head. These were my own private thoughts not yet tainted by people or circumstances. Approval wasn't required. Yet, in my immaturity I didn't let God in on my plans either. Like some dreamers, I thought the idea sounded good, so why wouldn't it work?

As I grew older my dreams changed to inventing and having my own business someday. I can remember working with my brother on a design to make bathing easier for special needs and handicapped individuals. We got as far as creating the prototype and experimenting with the device,

> **Genesis 37**
>
> [29]And Reuben returned unto the pit; and, behold, Joseph was not in the pit; and he rent his clothes.

Genesis 37

³⁰And he returned unto his brethren, and said, the child is not; and I, whither shall I go?

but since we lived in different states it was difficult to work out the kinks and the idea soon fizzled.

Even as a young adult, I still hadn't learned how to include my personal life with my spiritual life. I identified partnerships with humans and not with God.

Side Bar Conversation

Who's Your Family?

I separated my biological family from my spiritual family. I listened to friends and family, but ignored the voice of my spiritual family: God. But I soon learned that the voices of my biological family and friends could not change my mediocre existence. Only God's voice could move me to a great way of living full and abundant.

Who have you been listening to?

Sure, I could talk to God easy enough at bedtime or during morning prayer, but I didn't allow my spiritual life to merge into the everyday routine of life for completeness. Fulfilling the basic needs of life isn't the abundant life that God wants for me. I had mastered maintaining a career, being a wife, and taking care of the kids, but even a sleepwalker can maneuver through the house and complete normal routine tasks. Now, more than ever, I wanted to be awakened and I wanted to intertwine my dreams with a calling to do something for God. I wanted a calling to life - an abundant life.

> *Genesis 37*
>
> [31] And they took Joseph's coat, and killed a kid of the goats, and dipped the coat in the blood;

What dreams have you pursued that were outside of the will of God? Have you partnered with someone that

Genesis 37

³²And they sent the coat of many colours, and they brought it to their father; and said, this have we found: know now whether it be thy son's coat or no.

didn't share your values or did you date the hot and sexy guy when God said no?

Add your thought and comments below.

_____

_____

_____

_____

_____

_____

_____

_____

Remember when Isaac prayed to God on behalf of his wife Rebekah because she couldn't have children? The Lord answered his prayer and revealed to Rebekah that the older one would serve the younger one. Instead of trusting God, Rebekah took matters into her own hands, tricking Isaac into believing he was blessing Esau when he actually blessed Jacob.

Do you really think God wanted Rebekah to behave manipulatively? Yet, in spite of her selfish motives God still allowed the plan to work out and to accomplish what He intended. God had spoken His truth into existence regarding the twins and truth only requires cooperation with time to bring God's spoken Word to reality. Just like Rebekah, I was impatient and left the main ingredient of life out of the recipe: God. But God's plan for me would happen in spite of myself.

An example of leaving out the main ingredient happened during my high school years. My mom would sometimes leave

Genesis 37

[33] And he knew it, and said, it is my son's coat; an evil beast hath devoured him; Joseph is without doubt rent in pieces.

> **Genesis 37**
>
> [34] And Jacob rent his clothes, and put sackcloth upon his loins, and mourned for his son many days.

cooking instructions on how to finish a meal. On one occasion during the Thanksgiving holiday, my mom asked me to chop up a cup of bell peppers for the stuffing. I started working with great anticipation. As instructed, I mixed the peppers into the stuffing and baked it for the specified time. Before mealtime, my mom checked to see how the stuffing tasted. She immediately discovered that I had used jalapeno peppers instead of green peppers. For some families spicy stuffing would have been a big hit, but for my family this was a disaster.

Experience is the teacher. If you study under a great cook he may instruct you to sample the concoction as you go along to determine the right combinations of ingredients. Regardless of the cooking process, as a beginner, you wouldn't make a move without consulting the Expert.

I have since found out that the same is true with God. You shouldn't start your day, began a project, engage in a business deal, or make a family decision without God's approval to proceed. The main ingredient in life is God guiding you through the aid of the Holy Spirit. Your life recipe is a flop without Him.

Add your thought and comments below.

Genesis 37

[35] And all his sons and all his daughters rose up to comfort him; but he refused to be comforted; and he said, for I will go down into the grave unto my son mourning. Thus his father wept for him.

_____

_____

_____

_____

_____

The Main Ingredient
Brenette Wilder

Genesis 37

³⁶And the Midianites sold him into Egypt unto Potiphar, an officer of Pharaoh's, and captain of the guard

Scripture: Jeremiah 31:3
The LORD appeared to us in the past, saying, "I have loved you with an everlasting love; I have drawn you with loving-kindness."

Stir it up!
Inflame your inner man
God declares, Stir it up!
Listen to the utterance
God declares, Stir it up!
Be filled with the Holy Spirit
God declares, Stir it up!

With confidence
And faith and boldness to follow
Led by the Spirit
God declares to stir it up!

Chapter 4
The Voice, the Hunger, the List

"The Voice: How Does God Get Your Attention?"

*I*t's amazing how God uses everything around us to communicate His thoughts. Can you imagine hearing what you thought was a prompting from God while conducting a literature search in the library or while in the checkout line of the grocery store? I bet the girl at the library had no idea her search for information on erratic dreams would put me on a course to achieve my dream.

I can imagine her sleepless night the day before, tossing and turning unable to fall

Genesis 39

[1]And Joseph was brought down to Egypt; and Potiphar, an officer of Pharaoh, captain of the guard, an Egyptian, bought him of the hands of the Ishmeelites, which had brought him down thither.

> **Genesis 39**
>
> ²And the LORD was with Joseph, and he was a prosperous man; and he was in the house of his master the Egyptian.

asleep after having a dream that didn't make any sense to her. The randomness of events was significant enough to cause her to question the meaning of the dream and sent her on a quest to find an answer. On one side of town, a person is having an erratic dream while on the other side of town a dream desire is being resurrected. Yet, God's timing and sovereignty caused two events to coincide for a purpose.

God's timing is perfect, but ours is not. What are you trusting and waiting for God to do? Add your thoughts below.

_____

_____

_____

_____

| Dream Number 4 | Page 49 |

Why is it so difficult to wait on God?

Genesis 41

[1] And it came to pass at the end of two full years that Pharaoh dreamed: and, behold, he stood by the river.

_____

_____

_____

_____

_____

_____

_____

_____

_____

"The Hunger"

And then there was the magazine I read while standing in the checkout line of the grocery store. A story featured on the front cover caught my eye "Dream Big—How to Let Yourself Get What You Want." Turning to the story, the first thing I noticed was the subtitle included a question, "When's your

> **Genesis 41**
>
> ² And, behold, there came up out of the river seven kind, well-favored and fat-fleshed; and they fed in the reed-grass.

ship coming in?" Now this got my attention. In my own way, I was beginning to hear His voice softly, gently, and, yes, surprisingly calling me to this purpose. Talk about being starved! I was hungry for a real encounter with God. For once I didn't have to ask, "God, is this idea yours or is it mine?"

In the past, I thought God was saying "no" to my requests. Many times I thought, maybe God wanted me to be satisfied with the hand I had been dealt, or maybe I wasn't mature enough yet. Maybe all I should do is sit back and ride out life without complaining. God's responses of "no" and "wait" may very well have been true, but while I was waiting my hunger for something more didn't diminish. I would be lying if I said I didn't desire material things, but I wanted spiritual things more.

No one knew the need within me but God. It was hidden by a false impression that I had everything in order. It is a deep secret we all keep from each other. Why not break our silence. Let every Christian know up front that regardless of where you are in your relationship with God you long for it to be even closer.

"The List"

When we were asked to write down our list of dreams at the women's retreat, we were told to make a list without boundaries. In hindsight, I believe I limited my dream list because I knew I had to share my list with everyone in the room. I didn't want everyone knowing personal things about me. It was hard enough learning to open up to

Genesis 41

[3] And, behold, seven other kind came up after them out of the river, ill-favored and lean-fleshed, and stood by the other kind upon the brink of the river.

> **Genesis 41**
>
> [4] And the ill-favored and lean-fleshed kind did eat up the seven well-favored and fat kind. So Pharaoh awoke.

God about them. So I listed five things—

1) Learn a foreign language.

2) Learn to swim.

3) Take a cooking class.

4) Write a short story.

5) Take a gardening class.

Simple enough list all right, but for me completing everything on the list was tough. The list might as well have been narrowed to one thing: Take a trip to the moon. How would I ever make the time to do everything on my list or even one thing? Thanks to God, He knew where He wanted me to start. This book was the one thing that didn't require time away from home or initial startup money to begin. All I needed was paper, pencil, motivation, and confidence in God.

Dream Number 4

Add your thought and comments below.

Genesis 41

[5] And he slept and dreamed a second time: and, behold, seven ears of grain came up upon one stalk, rank and good.

Genesis 41

⁶ And, behold, seven ears, thin and blasted with the east wind, sprung up after them.

God's voice
Brenette Wilder

Scripture: 1 Kings 19:12
And after the earthquake there was a fire, but the Lord was not in the fire. And after the fire there was the sound of a gentle whisper.

Persistent, but not forceful
Continual, but not troublesome
Unrecognizable words, but not chatter
Faint. It is the voice of God

A whisper in the early morning
As sweet as a ripen fruit
Overflowing with juice and substance
To nourish your soul
Sweetness in His voice
Sweetness inputted in me
Sweetness surrounding me
Sweetness I return to Him

In praise and with a loud shout
You are worthy to be praised!

You are the creator of the world
You are worthy to be praised!

Your hands are mighty and strong
You are worthy to be praised!

You are my healer
You are worthy to be praised!

You are my redeemer
You are worthy to be praised!

You are my provider
You are worthy to be praised!

You are my dream keeper
You are worthy to be praised!

Genesis 41

[7] And the thin ears swallowed up the seven rank and full ears. And Pharaoh awoke, and, behold, it was a dream.

Chapter 5

Dream Fear Factors

Genesis 41

⁸ And it came to pass in the morning that his spirit was troubled; and he sent and called for all the magicians of Egypt, and all the wise men thereof: and Pharaoh told them his dream; but there was none that could interpret them unto Pharaoh.

Have you ever had a nightmare and when you awoke you were scared to death? What about a dream that put so much fear into you, it made you afraid to go back to sleep. On one occasion after praying to God about a personal problem, one individual in my dream walked by and touched me. I awoke thinking that I actually felt the touch. I awoke afraid and confused. I experienced that same inescapable feeling at the beginning stages of my journey to write – fear. Fear reared its ugly head and caused me to become afraid. I wondered if professional writers would criticize my writings. I could see book club groups giving my book a poor rating. A ball and chain, called fear, dragged behind me like a loyal friend, and I fought to loose each link, one by one, because fear would not control me.

It's funny how fear of trying new things can cause you to remember difficulties from your past. I believe Satan uses these hard times to stop you while God wants to use them to make you stronger. In stead of focusing on how you were successful, Satan tricks you into remembering the stumbling blocks. In my case, coming from the south, I spoke with a southern dialect when I first started College. My College English professors told me I wrote like I talked.

I thought I spoke well compared to some

Genesis 41

[9] Then spake the chief butler unto Pharaoh, saying, I do remember my faults this day.

> **Genesis 41**
>
> [10] Pharaoh was wroth with his servants, and put me in ward in the house of the captain of the guard, me and the chief baker:

of my associates. But, even though my dialect has improved I still say things that only a true Southerner would accept as proper English. It's amazing that I still remember my English professors' comments. Satan does his job well and will use just the right situation to stop your progress or constantly remind you of your past. But, my Pastor, Rev. George Ervin, once said when Satan reminds you of your past, you remind him of his future. It took some effort but I loosed that link from the chain.

After experiencing an awakening of confidence, I reminded myself that I could do all things through Christ that called me to a purpose for Him. My Pastor has said numerous times, "Sometimes you have to think yourself glad". He was right. It just didn't happen automatically for me. One day I even rehearsed the lines my husband would use to encourage the children, referring to the little red train. The phrase started with "I think I can" and continued to "I know I can." Sounds pretty elementary to some of you, but I did what it took to elude the threat of failure. I knew it wouldn't take much to sidetrack me.

Looking back that's why I didn't tell my family what I was planning. Too many times in fun they would jokingly say things that might kindle in me the wrong thoughts or emotions. My husband with good and practical intentions would lecture me about a business plan or an outline. On occasions he asked questions like, "Who will help you?" or "Do you have experience in that area?"

Genesis 41

[11] And we dreamed a dream in one night, I and he; we dreamed each man according to the interpretation of his dream

Genesis 41

[12] And there was with us there a young man, a Hebrew, servant to the captain of the guard; and we told him, and he interpreted to us our dreams; to each man according to his dream he did interpret.

Quite frankly, I am aware of the importance of a business plan and an outline, but I just didn't want to hear it. In order to make this dream happen I needed the confidence of God. I needed to avoid roadblocks and people blocks, and I needed to resist negative thinking. Yes, you need an outline. Yes, you need a business plan. But more importantly for me, I needed God! I knew the importance of family support, and after I had prayed and gained confidence in myself, I finally told them all about my plans.

My family was supportive but God's approval took precedence over their opinions.

Layers of my heart
Brenette Wilder

Scripture: Deuteronomy 7:18
Thou shalt not be afraid of them: but shalt well remember what the LORD thy God did unto Pharaoh, and unto all Egypt.

Three layers of my heart
I guard against attack
Three layers of my heart
Fear cannot have

Fear cannot have faith
Faith is the substance of things hoped for,
The evidence of things not seen –Hebrew 11.1

Fear cannot have love
Nor height, nor depth,
Nor any other creature,
Will be able to separate us from the love of God,
Which is in Christ Jesus our Lord – Romans 8:39

Fear cannot have my purpose
We know that all things work together for good to them that love God,
to them who are the called according to His purpose – Romans 8:28

Genesis 41

[13] And it came to pass, as he interpreted to us, so it was; me he restored unto mine office, and him he hanged.

Chapter 6
Don't Waste Time

Genesis 41

¹⁴ Then Pharaoh sent and called Joseph, and they brought him hastily out of the dungeon: and he shaved himself, and changed his raiment, and came in unto Pharaoh.

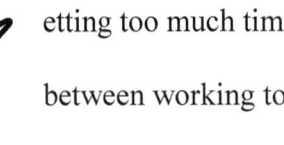etting too much time lapse between working towards your dream may cause you to lose momentum and focus. It's been a few weeks since I've picked up a pen to write. But today I am on a flight from my hometown with 45 minutes to write my thoughts. This time I know what needs to be said. I just left my brother who is battling cancer. His last medical report wasn't good; cancer has now spread to his brain. I couldn't help but remember the last medical emergency he experienced. His medical problems then just start with cancer. During a high school

football game he had an accident that left him a quadriplegic. Recovery was hard, but he managed to make the most of his life. Now another life and death situation is at hand. I am reminded about how important it is to live life fully without delay. About three years ago I started telling my brother that he had a story to tell. At least three to four times a year I would send him an email message reminding him to get started. The message would simply say: "It's time to tell your story." I felt that his courage to face life's challenges, of paralysis and now cancer, was a story that could help a great number of people. Even though I tried to make this a goal for him, I now realize he had already set and accomplished so many great goals that have inspired many of our

Genesis 41

[15] And Pharaoh said unto Joseph, I have dreamed a dream, and there is none that can interpret it: and I have heard say of thee, that thou canst understand a dream to interpret it.

> **Genesis 41**
>
> [16] And Joseph answered Pharaoh, saying, It is not in me: God shall give Pharaoh an answer of peace.

family members. My brother had accomplished so many things that had been closed to many disabled individuals. Completing his education (GED and vocational training) after a football accident paralyzed him, moving into an apartment and living alone, traveling, and even marrying were tremendous accomplishments. He didn't waste any time breaking down those quadriplegic barriers that would have brought many of us to a screeching halt. My brother got busy and stayed busy at life. The point I am trying to make is don't waste precious time. Life has funny twists and turns. There will be many times you won't be able to see around your problems. Angles that will make it difficult to navigate or work on your dreams.

A prime example of not accomplishing a fun and personal goal occurred on one of our vacations. The incident caused me to miss out on a once in a lifetime experience. My family and I were at the Grand Canyon and noticed people taking the path to the bottom of the Canyon. It was late, but we spontaneously decided to walk as far as we could down the Canyon. After a short time on the path, we came to what looked like a 90 degree turn. The path shrunk to nothing as it turned, and I envisioned the worst. My mind told me no way I was going around there. I got nervous and convinced my husband to turn back. Years later, I realized that decision to turn back was driven by fear. Our fun was cut short by my fear. So we have no satisfying memory of walking to the

> **Genesis 41**
>
> [17]And Pharaoh said unto Joseph, In my dream, behold, I stood upon the bank of the river:

Genesis 41

¹⁸And, behold, there came up out of the river seven kind, fat fleshed and well favoured; and they fed in a meadow:

end of that path.

> **In Loving Memory:**
>
> In October 2004, my brother passed away. I will miss him and will always remember the dreams we shared together. Don't miss out on life because you are afraid, have a handicap, or feel that you are too old. The time is now to live and to live abundantly.

Fear, procrastination, and self doubt will rob you of joy and happiness every time. They are enemies to your success.

Remember the following pointers:

1. Identify things that hinder you and prevent you from consistently working at your dreams.

2. Talk to God about these hindrances and pray to overcome them.

3. Develop a plan to overcome your hindrances.

Add your thought and comments below.

_____

_____

_____

_____

_____

Stop Your Excuses
Brenette Wilder

Scripture: Numbers 11:1
And when the people complained, it displeased the LORD: and the LORD heard it; and his anger was kindled; and the fire of the LORD burnt among them, and consumed them that were in the uttermost parts of the camp.

Inhale life
Exhale whining

Enhance faith
Expose doubt

Stop your excuses
Renew your purpose

Get on board, Rejoin life
God will notice, A better you
You will notice, A better way of living

Genesis 41

[19] And, behold, seven other kine came up after them, poor and very ill favoured and lean fleshed, such as I never saw in all the land of Egypt for badness.

Chapter 7
Opportunity, Not Failure

Genesis 41

[20] And the lean and the ill favoured kind did eat up the first seven fat kind.

Sometimes our dreams seem elusive. The days can slip so easily into years and time seems to literally challenge us; taunting us with its ability to steal away our dreams. I believe this unseen and silent slippage can be broken. Faith is the key. Faith will help you believe that if God gave you a dream, He will help you complete it. So when you come up against that giant of a brick wall, or if you have a temporary lapse in confidence, don't see it as failure. You may even think, "Too much time has gone by so why even try." "I ask: Why not try?"

God gives us so many chances to come to Him for help. He gives so many new opportunities to start again.

Patiently He waits for you to come to Him, so He can show you His love, Isaiah 30:18. The Word states that He will conquer you to bless you. For the Lord is faithful to His promises. Blessed are all those who wait for Him to help him. Don't trust the lies of others, laziness, time, or even your negative thinking over God. In Isaiah 30, the children of Israel sought protection and help from Egypt instead of God to save them from their enemy. God's jealousy was so great He was going to allow calamity to come upon them if they did not return back to Him. God's statement of conquer was out of love.

Genesis 41

[21] And when they had eaten them up, it could not be known that they had eaten them; but they were still ill favoured, as at the beginning. So I awoke.

> **Genesis 41**
>
> ²²And I saw in my dream, and, behold, seven ears came up in one stalk, full and good:

Conquering you to bless you may mean that He will turn up the heat. Return to God and wait on Him. God wants so much to bless you.

We all need to motivate ourselves from time to time. When you stumble take time to give yourself positive feedback and corrective advice. In addition to prayer, think of ways to keep yourself motivated. Consider the following;

- Form a Dream Club to work together in achieving your goals.
- Talk and seek guidance from people that have your best interests at heart.
- Research and read material related to your dream.
- Consider taking a class.
- Give up a few hours of television each

day and replace that time with working on your dream.

- Make a checklist to keep you on track.
- Post your dream list in a visible spot as a constant reminder.
- Set realistic goals.

> **Genesis 41**
>
> [23] And, behold, seven ears, withered, thin, and blasted with the east wind, sprung up after them:

This is me, making a difference

Scripture: Galatians 6:10
As we have therefore opportunity, let us do good unto all men, especially unto them who are of the household of faith.

An excerpt from an Optimist Essay written by Charleen Wilder

I want to make a difference so that the kids that I see today don't continue on the destructive road that leads to default. That is exactly why I am going to be a Psychologist.

I will solve problems that are beneath the surface; not with drugs or medication but with words and the realization that what they're doing now isn't working. I will help them understand that to be happy with

> **Genesis 41**
>
> ²⁴And the thin ears devoured the seven good ears: and I told this unto the magicians; but there was none that could declare it to me.

themselves things need to change. If they are happy with themselves they won't need to go searching for acceptance in the wrong crowd.

If I help those teenagers then the fears that are burdening me regarding the future will be relieved. I won't have to fear for the future because the folly that is keeping my generation in shackles will have been smashed.

It seems there are two extremes of people accented in my generation: the go-get-ers and the ones that don't care. I want to make a difference so that the balance will be overwhelmingly in the go-get-er's favor.

Chapter 8

Teamwork

If I asked you to interpret something you dreamed, would you give an explanation based on your life experience, images you've seen, or written material? Consider this: A dream when given by God can only be revealed by God. God equipped you with certain gifts, skills, and talents to be used to help others and to live out your life's purpose. Therefore, I believe a dream given by God will most likely center on your life's purpose. My dream was a yearning, a nagging at the deepest core within me, placed there by God and could only be

> **Genesis 41**
>
> ²⁵And Joseph said unto Pharaoh, The dream of Pharaoh is one: God hath shewed Pharaoh what he is about to do.

> **Genesis 41**
>
> ²⁶The seven good kind are seven years; and the seven good ears are seven years: the dream is one.

satisfied by God. If my dream was not identified accurately or fully understood, I believe emptiness, a lack of satisfaction in my life's choices, and a lack of fulfillment would be left in its place.

Shoot for the stars. You can do anything you set your mind to. Set high goals. These phrases are words of wisdom we hear all the time. Our family and friends will often encourage us to be our best, do our best, and achieve our best.

What if we took that same advice and combined it with unity? What if the church body helped each person fulfill their dreams… dreams that align with God? What if the body functioned as one organism? Wouldn't the organism always act in the best interest of the body? So if the legs had a dream to be the fastest runner or the hands wanted to paint beautiful pictures, wouldn't the body work to help it?

The body working together to help each part achieve is not a new concept (I Corinthians 12), just one we seldom fully put into action. We infrequently love each other the way Christ loves us. His love and plan for us has depth of consideration to our uniqueness and yes, to His purpose. God said: "For I know the plans I have for you, says the Lord. They are plans for good and not for disaster, to give you a future and a hope" Jeremiah 29:11. You might have forgotten to work your dream, but God has not forgotten.

The old saying that two heads are better than one is sound council. Two guys

Genesis 41

[27] And the seven thin and ill favoured kind that came up after them are seven years; and the seven empty ears blasted with the east wind shall be seven years of famine.

Genesis 41

^{28}This is the thing which I have spoken unto Pharaoh: What God is about to do he sheweth unto Pharaoh.

working on their doctoral studies at Stanford University got together to create a better way to search the Internet. They created a search engine and a successful company called Google.

A football team can't win a game with a single player. Even the beauty of the universe isn't complete without the stars, the moon, galaxies, and planets. A good plan can be even better with diverse thinking and by combining different gifts or talents. Self driven plans may be limited in distance and momentum. What you're lacking your partner may possess.

Make a list of someone you can partner with. Adding God to your team would be a great strategy.

Add your thought and comments below.

Genesis 41

[29] Behold, there come seven years of great plenty throughout all the land of Egypt:

Teamwork is a woman

Genesis 41

³⁰And there shall arise after them seven years of famine; and all the plenty shall be forgotten in the land of Egypt; and the famine shall consume the land;

Scripture: Eph 4:16
From whom the whole body fitly joined together and compacted by that which every joint supplieth, according to the effectual working in the measure of every part, maketh increase of the body unto the edifying of itself in love.

Written in collaboration with Christina Wilder

Teamwork is sensitive to others.
She says my success is your success.
She works tirelessly and is not lazy.
She is a part of the clan, but does not dominate.

Teamwork is a woman.
Her words are sincere.
Her voice soft and commanding.
Her movement swift and sure.

Teamwork does her part;
And lets others know she sees them doing their part.
Teamwork seeks out the inner strengths;
And sees the inward person.

Teamwork conjures faith that moves mountains;
And achieves impossible odds.
I say again, Teamwork is a woman.

Chapter 9
Give Thanks

*I*t would be a violation of everything that I have been taught if I didn't set aside a chapter to emphasize the importance of giving thanks. Thanking God for empowering you to fulfill your destiny <u>must be</u> a priority. Start at the beginning when giving thanks. In my case, I began with thanking Him for all the circumstances that led me to my prayer closet. The visit to the library, the outreach project, and even the visit to the grocery store refueled the fire to Dream Number 4.

Make a list of personal or business problems that you struggled through during

Genesis 41

[31] And the plenty shall not be known in the land by reason of that famine following; for it shall be very grievous.

Genesis 41

³²And for that the dream was doubled unto Pharaoh twice; it is because the thing is established by God, and God will shortly bring it to pass.

the initial startup of your dream project, people that discouraged you, or even mental challenges you had to arrest. Thank God for allowing you to continue past those experiences. Your beginning point may be quite different than mine, but let God know you realized it was His strength that got you through and not your own.

Create your thanksgiving list below:

1. _____

_____

_____

2. _____

_____

_____

3. _____

_____

Some dreams may require money to get them off and running. Did God take care of every bill? Well praise Him for it! Did you receive support from family and friends? Make sure you let them know personally or write them a thank you note to show how much you appreciated their help. I am not the expert, but I believe that if you show thanksgiving in your life - then happiness, joy, peace of mind, and contentment may follow. How can a person be thankful and unhappy at the same time? Sounds like a pretty hard task. Stop now and give thanks to God.

Genesis 41

[33]Now therefore let Pharaoh look out a man discreet and wise, and set him over the land of Egypt.

Dream Number 4 | Page 82

Live for Me
Brenette Wilder

Genesis 41

³⁴Let Pharaoh do this, and let him appoint officers over the land, and take up the fifth part of the land of Egypt in the seven plenteous years.

Scripture: Psalm 100
Shout with joy to the Lord, all the earth!
Worship the Lord with gladness.
Come before Him, singing with joy.
Acknowledge that the Lord is God!
He made us, and we are His.
We are His people, the sheep of His pasture.
Enter His gates with thanksgiving; go into His courts with praise.
Give thanks to Him and praise His name.
For the Lord is good.
His unfailing love continues forever,
and His faithfulness continues to each generation.

Dig Deep!
This is your life
Live it fully
Live it abundantly
Live it for me

Dig Deep!
Don't compromise yourself
Live with integrity
Live it for me

Dig Deep!
Listen to me
Come into your purpose
Live it for me

Dream Number 4

Dig Deep!
Start a new chapter
What's taking so long?
Live for me.

Genesis 41

³⁵And let them gather all the food of those good years that come, and lay up corn under the hand of Pharaoh, and let them keep food in the cities.

Chapter 10
To Share, or Not To Share

Genesis 41

³⁶And that food shall be for store to the land against the seven years of famine, which shall be in the land of Egypt; that the land perish not through the famine.

Sharing your dream with others when it is in the draft stages of your mind will not always bring agreement and understanding. Others may judge your dream and your ability to achieve it, based on their limited interaction with you or their own limitations. If others can't see your dream, they cannot be convinced it will happen. Their acceptance begins and ends with "their" internal maturity level and external sight. I even read about brothers that didn't believe in their sibling's dream of being a great leader. I am sure they especially wouldn't have imagined it after they threw him into a pit followed by his imprisonment.

Your dream may foster jealousy, judgment, and cause division. Only you can authenticate your dream, with the aid of the Holy Spirit. Genesis 37 tells us Joseph's brothers were jealous of him and his relationship with their dad. After Joseph shared his dream that placed him in authority over them; his brothers only disliked him more.

Tread lightly. Do not be so quick to share information. It's not important that people around you know what you're planning. Wait for God to manifest it. The dream would most likely be received better after it is fulfilled. God's Word will not be wasted and is more than able to fulfill its purpose in due time.

> **Genesis 41**
>
> [37] And the thing was good in the eyes of Pharaoh, and in the eyes of all his servants.

Genesis 41

[38] And Pharaoh said unto his servants, Can we find such a one as this is, a man in whom the Spirit of God is?

Add your thought and comments below.

_____

_____

_____

_____

Courage
Brenette Wilder

Scripture: Deuteronomy 31:7
And Moses called unto Joshua, and said unto him in the sight of all Israel, Be strong and of a good courage: for thou must go with this people unto the land which the LORD hath sworn unto their fathers to give them; and thou shalt cause them to inherit it.

Speaking the undiluted truth.
Standing alone.
Smiling when your world is crumbling.
Silent suffering.
Surrendering when you are ahead.
Selfless Service.
Seeing yourself through the eyes of God.
Sharing when you have little to give.
Self Denial and Self Control.
Saving others while you are drowning.
Scaling back when you are operating with a skeleton's salary.
Self-adjustment when you need to change.

Chapter 11
Searching

I had been searching for my dream my whole life. Like Peter Pan sought after his shadow, I desired to know how God would build my future. I didn't know at the time, but my search was an inward search. It was a search to know God as He knew me. "God is intimately acquainted with all my ways. Even before there is a word on my tongue, behold, O Lord, thou doest know it all" Psalms 139:3. I can't get away from God; He knows everything about me and has invested time into knowing me in depth. He knows me better than my family, husband, and

Genesis 41

[39] And Pharaoh said unto Joseph, Forasmuch as God hath shewed thee all this, there is none so discreet and wise as thou art:

> **Genesis 41**
>
> ⁴⁰Thou shalt be over my house, and according unto thy word shall all my people be ruled: only in the throne will I be greater than thou.

friends. My heart's desire was really God's desire for me.

The dream you have is not your own and it won't be fulfilled for your own satisfaction. You dream's primary purpose is to satisfy God's will and the body of Christ.

Add your thought and comments below.

_____

_____

_____

_____

Searching

Scripture: Luke 19:10
For the Son of man is come to seek and to save that which was lost.

Written by Catera Wilder

Searching for the meaning of life;
by asking a flood of questions.
Questions that no one seems to know the answers to.

Traveling on life's journey;
with no map or destination.
Not sure what will happen next.

Dream Number 4

Trudging along the path;
Looking for anyone who can relate.
Meeting masked characters with a hidden agenda.
Gazing at glazed eyes that reveal a hurt too painful to penetrate.
Wondering if evolution has only produced surrogates of the human race.

Fed up with the emptiness that expands farther than the eye can see.
Thinking my answerless questions weren't meant to be asked.
Concluding that this lonely life wasn't meant for me.

A light shining from the distance interrupts my thoughts.

Through squinted eyes I see a figure.
From my blurry vision a man emerges.
A look of mercy and grace upon his face.
Calm and peace of mind flood my body.
The One who answers all questions.
The One who heals all hurt is here.

> **Genesis 41**
>
> [41] And Pharaoh said unto Joseph, See, I have set thee over all the land of Egypt.

Chapter 12

What's Next?

Genesis 41

⁴²And Pharaoh took off his ring from his hand, and put it upon Joseph's hand, and arrayed him in vestures of fine linen, and put a gold chain about his neck;

Take delight in the LORD, and He will give you the desires of your heart (Ps. 37:4). There is no invisible ceiling for dreamers. The sky is the limit. Gender or race will not be a hindrance before God. Obedience will be a prerequisite so align your dreams with His ways and Dream Big.

After walking through one open door, ask God what He wants from you next. Doors may be closed initially and "no" may be the response you hear, but continue to seek God until you are clear what you should be doing. Don't rush. Take time to listen and draw from your gifts and talents. God put them there for a reason. A closed door will give you time to get perspective. Don't allow yourselves to be comfortable with life being the same; God can use you in many different ways. His love says yes to life, yes to second chances, yes to hope, yes to you.

Genesis 41

[43] And he made him to ride in the second chariot which he had; and they cried before him, Bow the knee: and he made him ruler over all the land of Egypt.

September 5, 2009 update

Now I must share the honest truth. I am ashamed to tell you, but five years has passed and my writing has set in my closet unpublished. What Happened! I bet God is wondering if I had amnesia. Looking back I can only recall coming to a place where I thought the book was complete. I didn't feel like I had more to say. So, instead of publishing the book, a draft was neatly tuck

Genesis 41

[44] And Pharaoh said unto Joseph, I am Pharaoh, and without thee shall no man lift up his hand or foot in all the land of Egypt.

away and one day led to two days, followed by months, until a number of years had passed when I heard Elder Cathy Moffitt, from Heartfelt International Ministries speak at a local church. She stated, "Somebody in the audience has a dream."

I can't explain the delay in publishing this book, but it was not forgotten. Time can steal your youthfulness if not guarded. And can steal away your purpose. Stay as near to your dream as you can. Don't allow the gap of time to form a gorge that can't be forced back together. Who can restore lost time? Who can travel back to regain a moment you wish you had taken advantage of? No one can, but we can be good stewards of the time that God gives us.

In Elder Moffitt's speech she stated:

"When it is your time it will happen." Well the time is now. I pray that my life struggles to complete this dream will help you. I hope you realize that my life is not much different than yours. We all have the same tendencies to delay or stall, but I pray that you have stayed on task. Your journey may be long, intense, silent, and sometimes delayed as Elder Moffitt mentioned, but in the end you will be able to check off one thing you hoped for and **dreamed for!**

Add your thought and comments below.

Genesis 41

[45] And Pharaoh called Joseph's name Zaphnathpaaneah; and he gave him to wife Asenath the daughter of Potipherah priest of On. And Joseph went out over all the land of Egypt.

_____

_____

_____

_____

_____

Dream Number 4 | Page 94

Genesis 41

⁴⁶And Joseph was thirty years old when he stood before Pharaoh king of Egypt. And Joseph went out from the presence of Pharaoh, and went throughout all the land of Egypt.

My Past is Behind Me
Brenette Wilder

Scripture: Philippians 3:14
I press toward the mark for the prize of the high calling of God in Christ Jesus.

How do I put my past behind me?
By taking miniature strives with a clear vision of the future.
By exhausting every resource
As God opens each door.

Be satisfied with forward progressions.
Seek small achievements each day.
Focus your eyes on the horizon
And don't look behind.

Transform your thinking.
Know that you are a spirit in a human body.
Allow troubles to roll away
Like wave wakes behind you.

Let satisfaction find you.
Let God give you joy.
Let the sparkle in your eye overtake your heart.
Know that your future is bright.

Notes

About the Author

Brenette Wilder graduated from the University of Arkansas in Fayetteville with a Bachelor of Science in Chemical Engineering. As a working mother, she founded the nonprofit organization, **Kansas City Teen Summit**, which aims to engage at-risk youth in the urban community with educational, career and skill-building resources.

This book was written to fulfill her dream of writing for God, but most of the profit from this book will provide money to Kansas City Teen Summit. Brenette is a new writer who has been involved in youth ministry and is using one dream to support another dream … her dream of helping others.

www.ingramcontent.com/pod-product-compliance
Lightning Source LLC
Chambersburg PA
CBHW070646300426
44111CB00013B/2283